Samuel Skipper

The Politics of Immigration

Is Germany moving towards a Multicultural Society?

Anchor Academic Publishing

Skipper, Samuel: The Politics of Immigration. Is Germany moving towards a Multicultural Society?, Hamburg, Anchor Academic Publishing 2017

Buch-ISBN: 978-3-96067-102-2
PDF-eBook-ISBN: 978-3-96067-602-7
Druck/Herstellung: Anchor Academic Publishing, Hamburg, 2017

Bibliografische Information der Deutschen Nationalbibliothek:
Die Deutsche Nationalbibliothek verzeichnet diese Publikation in der Deutschen Nationalbibliografie; detaillierte bibliografische Daten sind im Internet über http://dnb.d-nb.de abrufbar.

Bibliographical Information of the German National Library:
The German National Library lists this publication in the German National Bibliography. Detailed bibliographic data can be found at: http://dnb.d-nb.de

All rights reserved. This publication may not be reproduced, stored in a retrieval system or transmitted, in any form or by any means, electronic, mechanical, photocopying, recording or otherwise, without the prior permission of the publishers.

Das Werk einschließlich aller seiner Teile ist urheberrechtlich geschützt. Jede Verwertung außerhalb der Grenzen des Urheberrechtsgesetzes ist ohne Zustimmung des Verlages unzulässig und strafbar. Dies gilt insbesondere für Vervielfältigungen, Übersetzungen, Mikroverfilmungen und die Einspeicherung und Bearbeitung in elektronischen Systemen.

Die Wiedergabe von Gebrauchsnamen, Handelsnamen, Warenbezeichnungen usw. in diesem Werk berechtigt auch ohne besondere Kennzeichnung nicht zu der Annahme, dass solche Namen im Sinne der Warenzeichen- und Markenschutz-Gesetzgebung als frei zu betrachten wären und daher von jedermann benutzt werden dürften.

Die Informationen in diesem Werk wurden mit Sorgfalt erarbeitet. Dennoch können Fehler nicht vollständig ausgeschlossen werden und die Diplomica Verlag GmbH, die Autoren oder Übersetzer übernehmen keine juristische Verantwortung oder irgendeine Haftung für evtl. verbliebene fehlerhafte Angaben und deren Folgen.

Alle Rechte vorbehalten

© Anchor Academic Publishing, Imprint der Diplomica Verlag GmbH
Hermannstal 119k, 22119 Hamburg
http://www.diplomica-verlag.de, Hamburg 2017
Printed in Germany

Contents

Introduction 3

Case Study and Structure 6

Chapter 1 Conceptual Framework: Citizenship, Integration, Assimilation
and Europeanization 8

    1.1 Citizenship 8

    1.2 Assimilationist Mode of Political Integration 9

    1.3 Europeanization 11

Chapter 2 Immigration in Germany: A Contradictory Policy Area 13

Chapter 3 Citizenship and Integration in Germany 19

    3.1 The 2000 Nationality Act 19

    3.2 The Leitkultur Debate: Assimilation or Integration? 23

Chapter 4 The Impact of Domestic and External pressure 30

    4.1 Demographic and Labour Shortage 31

    4.2 Europeanization of Immigration Policy and Identity? 33

Conclusion 37

Bibliography 40

Introduction

The topic of immigration is never simple. Questions such as 'who belongs to society?' and 'how do you define national identity?', or 'what values are needed to maintain a coexisting society?' are extremely difficult to answer. Global migration introduces unprecedented challenges for conceptualising the integration of immigrants. Moreover, as Brett Klopp suggests, "while no one has yet produced a general theory of immigration per se, immigration has become a permanent feature of our modern and increasingly globalising world."[1] In fact, at the start of the new century, immigration has undoubtedly become one of the most relevant and pressing issues in the European Union. Each year, the average number of the immigrant population arriving in the EU reaches the mark of two and a half million.[2] In 2001, over 70% of the increase in the EU's population came from cross-border migration. Italy and Germany accounted for 17 per cent each of all the net migration within the EU.[3] In a somewhat paradoxical way, most countries across the Old Continent have adopted a 'policy mix' by trying to restrict foreign recruitment and at the same time move towards a more open society. On the one hand, European states are keen to open their borders to capital, goods and services, while on the other hand attempt to filter the movement of people by making a distinction between wanted and unwanted migration. In an era of 'hypercapitalism',[4] in which capitalism has strengthened itself by becoming the prevailing mode of production around the world, forcing domestic economies to constantly adapt to global competitive conditions, states seek to encourage economic migration in order to sustain the demands of the domestic economy. Yet, increased worldwide interconnectedness and the new patterns of migration and settlement promoted by the process of globalisation have lead to the emergence of a vigorous debate about the rise of a multicultural society. As Samuel Huntington famously pointed out, "cultural characteristics and differences are less mutable and hence less easily compromised and resolved than political and economic ones."[5] Hence, Western Europeans fear that large scale immigration

---

[1] Klopp B. 'German multiculturalism: immigrant integration and the transformation of citizenship' (2002, Connecticut: Praeger Publishers) p 8
[2] Heywood. P. Et al, 'Developments in European Politics,' (London,2006: Palgrave Macmillan) p 281
[3] Eurostat '379.4 million inhabitants in the EU and 305.1 million in the euro zone on 1 January 2002' http://epp.eurostat.ec.europa.eu/cache/ITY_PUBLIC/3-11012002-AP/EN/3-11012002-AP-EN.HTML Accessed on 14/08/09
[4] See Scholte J.A. 'Globalisation: a critical introduction' (2005,London: Palgrave Macmillan)
[5] Huntington S. 'The Clash of Civilizations?' *Foreign Affairs*, Vo. 72, No. 3 (Summer 1993) p 27

may lead to "irrevocable" changes that would threaten the "historically given self-perceptions of European nations."[6] Consequently, the debates on immigration have shifted from an economic discourse to more central interrelated question of permanent settlement, nationality, citizenship and integration. Questions on membership and the rights of immigrants and ethnic minorities have assumed a central role in discussions on national identity in the aftermath of the Cold War. The emphasis on national identity is particularly strong in Germany where a large minority believes that *Volkervermischung* (mixing of peoples) should be avoided in order to keep the German people 'pure'. In contrast to traditional settler societies such as the United States of America and Australia characterised by a civic and more liberal understanding of nationality, Germany " more easily conceive of a nation or people as an aggregate existing independent of state organisation, unified by certain commonalities such as language, religion, culture, history, and descent."[7] Yet, from the beginning of the Cold War up to today, Germany has been the country with the largest foreign population in Europe. Over the last fifty years, the Federal Republic of Germany has been the destination of about thirty million immigrants, many of whom have taken the decision to settle permanently. Eurostat statistics reveal that around 11 million people have entered Germany between 1991 and 2000.[8] If in 1960 the foreign population was constituted by fewer than 700,000 persons, today the number has risen to almost 7.3 million foreign inhabitants, representing 9 per cent of the total population.[9] In 2006, over fifteen million people in Germany – roughly one every five residents – turned out to possess a migrant background.[10] On a European scale, Germany can be said to represent the first destination for immigrants since unification in 1989. On a global level, Germany is the second largest immigrant receiving country after the United States. Nevertheless, only recently has Germany recognised and admitted that it is an ethnically and culturally diverse

---

[6] Hammar T. 'Comparing European and North American International Migration', *International Migration View*, Vo. 23 No. 3 (1989) p 637

[7] Neuman G. 'Nationality Law in the United States and Germany' in Schuck P. & Munz R. 'In paths to Inclusion: The integration of Migrants in the United States and Germany' (1998, Providence: Berghan Books) p 249-250

[8] Eurostat 'Eurostat '379.4 million inhabitants in the EU and 305.1 million in the euro zone on 1 January 2002' http://epp.eurostat.ec.europa.eu/cache/ITY_PUBLIC/3-11012002-AP/EN/3-11012002-AP-EN.HTML Accessed on 14/08/09

[9] Ibid

[10] 'Deutschland: 15 Mio. Einwohner mit 'Migrationshintergrund' Migration und Bevolkerung 5 2006 http://www.migration-info.de/migration_und_bevoelkerung/artikel/060502.htm Accessed on 14/08/09

society. Before the 1998 elections, successive governments have always stuck to the maxim that Germany is 'not a country of immigration.'

The infamous phrase came under increased pressure with the electoral victory of the Red-Green coalition in 1998. New laws regarding immigration, integration and citizenship were on the agenda with the aim of replacing the traditional ethnocultural model of German nationhood with a more liberal and modern model by moving away from the concepts of Volk and *ius sanguinis*. The conservative CDU, however, accused the Schroder government of trying to jeopardize German cultural identity, causing a fierce debate known as the Leitkultur (Guiding culture) debate. On the one side of this debate there were the conservative CDU politicians who viewed Germany in ethno-nationalist terms, while on the other members of the Green Party and the SPD, who attempted substituting the 'volkish' tradition with a multicultural model of citizenship that guaranteed universal human rights.

The aim of this study is to assess which of these two models are currently prevailing in moulding immigration and integration policy. Has the progressive left achieved its objective of moving away from the traditional ethnocultural and assimilationalist model defining citizenship towards a more inclusive multicultural model[11]? This study will argue that the ethno-cultural and assimilationalist model is still succeeding because even though Germany's policies on immigration have undergone significant and unprecedented changes, Rogers Brubaker's claim that the "automatic transformation of immigrants into citizens remains unthinkable in Germany" [12] still appears depicting the current political and social reality. The first hypothesis is that immigrants are still expected to assimilate rather than integrate. To test this argument or hypothesis, evidence will be taken from both the 2000 Nationality Act and contemporary debates over citizenship to suggest that immigrants are still expected to assimilate German culture rather than integrate. At the same time, however, the policies on immigration and citizenship undertaken by the red-green coalition have eliminated the 'not a country of immigration' maxim from political discourse and represent a first step towards replacing the ethnocultural model. In fact, the study will also

---

[11] Note- This study is not going to focus on the term multiculturalism itself. I will treat multiculturalism as a term used by the German left parties as a means to describe the alternative model to the ethnocultural model based on the recognition of different cultures in society.

[12] Brubaker W.R. 'Citizenship and Nationhood in France and Germany' (1992, Cambridge, Mass: Harvard University Press) p 185

argue that the traditional ethnocultural-assimilationalist model will most likely not endure in the foreseeable future because important domestic pressures, such as demographic and skill shortages, and external factors like the European Union will eventually force Germany to adopt a more civic and pluralistic model characterising countries such as Britain, France, Sweden, and the Netherlands. The second hypothesis is that endogenous factors and the Europeanization of both national identity and immigration policy-making will have an increasing impact on Germany society and the ethnocultural notion of citizenship. To test this second hypothesis, evidence will be taken from statistical data and figures on demographic and skill shortages, while the effect of Europeanization will be assessed by discussing the Treaty on European Union in Maastricht and the Treaty of Amsterdam.

Case Study and Structure

Germany has been chosen as a case study for various reasons. Firstly, since reunification immigration and asylum have been a matter of concern for the German public and have always been at the centre of attention during successive political elections at the national and local level. The Politbarometer (Forschungsgruppe Wahlen) surveys show that today *Auslanderpolitik* is still viewed as the most pressing political problem. Opinion Polls show that the vast majority of the German public continues to preserve its negative attitudes and sentiments towards immigrants and opposes the idea of granting citizenship to foreigners.[13] As Anetta Kahane, one of Germany's best-known anti-racism campaigners asserted in an interview, unlike much of the Western world "there's absolutely no understanding in Germany of the concept of integration and coexistence of different cultures."[14] At the same time, however, the integration of immigrants in society is an extremely sensitive topic given the Nazi legacy and the infamous behaviour towards non-Germans. Secondly, the German concepts of nationality and identity are different from other 'classic' immigration countries in Western Europe based on a civic model of citizenship. Finally, the final part of this study is going to discuss the role of domestic pressures as well as the various aspects of Europeanization and their potential impact in Germany. Thus, Germany has been chosen as

---

[13] Note- Precise statistics will be provided in Ch 3
[14] Deutsche Welle 'Germany's Long Road to Multiculturalism' 21.07.2005

a single case study since a cross-national analysis would divert the focus and would risk becoming overly stretched.

The first part of the study is going to clarify some of the concepts which are going to be used while analysing the German case. These include interrelated concepts including citizenship, integration, assimilation, and Europeanization. This should help provide a conceptual framework. The second section will briefly analyse the historical traditions and dynamics of immigration and integration in Germany. In order to fully understand current policy decisions and political debates, it is essential to be familiar with the historical legacy of a country, which pushes governments into a 'path dependency.' In fact, as Peters points out, "when a government programme or organisation embarks on a path there is an inertial tendency for those initial policy choices to persist. The path may be altered, but it requires a good deal of political pressure to produce the change."[15] The third part will then analyse one of the most important policies on immigration crafted by the Schroder government, the 2000 Nationality Act. As Green put it, "as well as immigration, residence and citizenship policy standing out for their importance in German politics as a whole, the policy sector per se is quite unlike any other in the domestic politics of industrialised countries" since it concentrates exclusively on non-citizens.[16] As the analysis of the Leitkultur debate will show, the contents and the effects of this reform had important implications on the concept of citizenship, but have not completely transformed its ethnocultural characteristic. The final section is going to assess the role of the European Union and the demographic/skill shortages in acting as a dynamic force affecting domestic policy on immigration and inducing the re-conceptualisation of the concept of *Staatsvolk*. For instance, would a European 'policy framework' allow the harmonisation of issues related to immigration such as citizenship laws and dual nationality? Would this encourage Germany move towards a civic model like most of its European counterparts?

---

[15] Peters G. 'Institutional Theory in Political Science: The New Institutionalism' (London, 1999: Pinter) p 63
[16] Green S. 'The politics of exclusion: Institutions and immigration policy in contemporary Germany' (2004, Manchester University Press) 4

Chapter 1 Conceptual Framework: Citizenship, Integration, Assimilation and Europeanization

1.1 Citizenship

Immigration, integration, and the acquisition of citizenship are an interrelated process. The act of acquisition of citizenship is viewed as a fundamental step of the migratory process and as an indicator that helps to assess the level of integration of the immigrant population in the receiving country. The benefits of German citizenship include: "access to the German as well as all the EU labour markets, unrestricted access to the health and welfare system, any wage premium paid by discriminating employers to citizens, increased worldwide mobility, the right to vote and be elected in Germany and the EU, and the right to own property in Germany and the EU."[17] As Gerarld Neuman point out, "citizenship carries the potential for empowerment, through voting, through government service, through military service and the accompanying social respect."[18]

The notion of citizenship, which can be defined as "the set of rights, duties, and identities linking citizens to the nation-state,"[19] is of fundamental importance in the construction of national identity. At the same time, national identity still plays a primary role in the acquisition of those legal prerequisite necessary for the attainment of political rights. Thus, even though conceptually nationality and citizenship can be separated, practically they are inextricably linked to each other. Before the reforms carried out by the Red-Green coalition via the 2000 Nationality Act, German citizenship was firmly rooted in the 1913 Nationality Law. The 1913 Reich *Staatsangehorigekeitsgesetz* defined nationality based on the principle of *ius sanguinis*- or descent by blood- according to which a potential member must embrace the ethno-cultural characteristic of the German community, with little regard for birthplace and residence. Madel rightly affirms that "the confluence of German laws of citizenship and ideologies of ethnicity, nation and state, have effectively prevented this population [Turkish

---

[17] Kahanec M. & Tosun M.S. 'Political Economy of Immigration in Germany: Attitudes and Citizenship Aspirations' *Institute for the Study of Labour (IZA)* No 3140 November 2007 p 3

[18] Neuman G.L. 'National Law as a Method of Integration – A Comparison Between the USA and Germany' draft chapter p 4

[19] Koopmans R. & Statham P. 'Migration and ethnic relations as a field of political contention: An opportunity structure approach' in Koopman R. & Statham P. 'Challenging Immigration and Ethnic Relations Politics: Comparative European Perspective' (2000,Oxford: Oxford University Press) p 28

Community] from achieving legal and social equality, and civil rights, by denying them crucial access to full citizenship."[20] The Nationality Law based on ethnographic notions of citizenship was modernised and partly liberalised with the introduction of *Ius soli* (citizenship based on territory), but the transition towards a more civic model is still by large incomplete. The failure of introducing dual citizenship signifies that citizenship is still conceived not only as a type of membership, but also as "a specific cultural imprint on nationhood, which functions as a form of symbolic closure restricting, albeit to different extents and under nationally specific conditions, the ability of migrants to join the national community."[21] Nationhood, is still viewed by the conservatives not as the holder of universal political values, but as an "organic cultural linguistic community; the nationhood is constituted by ethnocultural unity."[22] Consequently, as Brett Klopp provocatively argued, "nearly fifty years after the Holocaust it appeared that Germany was still a country only for the Germans." [23] These notions of nationhood and citizenship somewhat still imply that the assimilation of immigrants is an essential prerequisite of integration policy.

1.2 Assimilationalist Mode of Political Integration

Numerous various and distinct modes or patterns of national integration exist. Exploring these different national patterns would go beyond the primary intent of this study that is establishing whether the citizenship reform in 2000 was successful in eradicating the ethnographic notion of nationhood. Broadly speaking integration implies adaptation and, in the words of Simon Green, it "consists of both immigrant and host society modifying their behaviour around universally accepted norms and standards."[24] Assimilation, on the other hand, can be described as the 'process of making similar' and involves complete absorption. The assimilationalist mode of political integration, mostly advocated by conservatives and nationalists, views the nation state as the cornerstone of its thinking and is based on the

---

[20] Madel R. ' Fortress Europe and the Foreigners Within: Germany's Turks' in Goddard V.A. & Llobera J.R. and Shore C. The Anthropology of Europe (Oxford: Berg, 1994) p 117
[21] Koopmans R. & Statham P. ' 2000 p 29
[22] Brubaker W.R. 'Citizenship and Nationhood in France and Germany' (1992, Cambridge, Mass: Harvard University Press) p 17
[23] Klopp B.'German Multiculturalism: Immigrant Integration and the Transformation of Citizenship' (Westport: Praeger Publishers, 2002)
[24] Green S. In Padgett S. Paterson W.E. Smith G. 2003 p 244

belief that no polity can be durable and consistent without a community sharing a common national culture.[25] Cultural and ethnic minorities are expected to assimilate into the dominant national culture by embracing the host society's way of life, common values, moral beliefs and social practices and at the same time abandoning their separate culture. In sum, "if they wish to become part of society and be treated like the rest of their fellow-citizens, they should assimilate. If they insist on retaining their separate cultures, they should not complain if they are viewed as outsiders and subjected to discriminatory treatment."[26] It can be argued that policies based on assimilation seldom work because they are likely to reinforce and increase differences between members of society instead of alleviating them by causing a reaction to the assimilatory pressures. As Parekh notes, "when a society refuses to accommodate the legitimate demands of its cultural minorities, the latter seek to exploit such spaces as society itself provides to legitimize their demands."[27] The Leitkultur debate will show that nevertheless the mentality according to which 'if immigrants want a place in our society they should become just like us' is still widespread in German society. As Green pointed out, "Germany's approach meant that immigrants were expected not to integrate, but to assimilate: that is, to give up the majority of their cultural identity in favour of becoming (not just legally) German."[28]

However, it is extremely important to specify that even if this exclusive approach to identity and citizenship was the cause for the incomplete membership status of the immigrant population in Germany, yet the lack of political and cultural integration did not exclude social integration. German migrants have been famously defined 'denizens' since they possessed legal and social, but not political rights. The main element of distinction between citizens and 'semi-citizens' or 'quasi citizens' is in fact the access to political rights, which are essential because "it is those with the right to vote and to be voted for may make, amend, and repeal the laws, including those concerning citizenship and naturalisation criteria."[29] Thus, even though this study will mostly focus on the cultural and political dimension of integration since these are viewed as key in the process of becoming full

---

[25] Parekh B. 'Rethinking Multiculturalism' (New York:Palgrave Macmillan 2006) 196-197
[26] Ibid
[27] Ibid p 198
[28] Green S. Cited in Padgett S.; Paterson W.E.; Smith G. 'Developments in German politics'(London: Palgrave Macmillan 2003) p 245
[29] Klopp Brett 2002 p14

members of society, we must not forget that in Germany a lot of the focus is centred on social integration within the welfare state. In the words of Frank Eckardt, "German integration is specifically organized within the framework of the universalist welfare state" and "political integration was always understood as the 'pinnacle' of social integration and not as an end in itself."[30]

1.3 Europeanization

At the start of the new century, the European dimension is an important source of domestic policy framework, including *Auslanderpolitik*. As Bendel affirmed, "in some important areas national asylum and immigration policy has long become unthinkable without the EU."[31] Europeanization has been successful in asylum and refugee policies, an area that has traditionally been linked to national sovereignty. But how do you conceptualise the term? There are many 'faces' of Europeanization. A useful definition to provide a framework has been offered by Bulmer and Radaelli:

"processes of construction, diffusion and institutionalisation of formal and informal rules, procedures, policy paradigms, styles, 'ways of doing things' and shared beliefs and norms which are first defined and consolidated in the EU policy process and then incorporated in the logic of domestic discourse, political structures and public policies."[32]

Europeanization is the "development of EU policies in particular, issue-areas embodying new rules, norms, regulations, and procedures."[33] Hence, the process of Europeanization of immigration can be assessed by the amount of EU directives and regulations regarding immigration policies like for instance a common asylum system. This thesis views Europeanization as the impact of the European Union on the member states. The extent of the European impact on national immigration policy reforms is difficult to agree on.

---

[30] Eckardt F. 'Multiculturalsim in Germany: From Ideology to Pragmatism- and Back?' *National Identities* Vol. 9 No. 3 September 2007 p237

[31] Bendel P. 'Immigration Policy in the European Union: Still bringing up the walls for fortress Europe?' Migration Letters Vo 2 N.1 April 2005 p 22

[32] Bulmer S.J. & Radaelli C.M. 'The Europeanisation of National Policy?' *Queen's Papers on Europeanisation* Vo. 1 2004 p 4

[33] Risse 'A European Identity' in Cowles G.M.; Caporaso J.; Risse T.' Transforming Europe' (Cornell: Cornell University Press, 2001) p 218

Different scholars provide different and sometimes contradictory evidence on how policy on a European level can affect domestic politics of immigration. According to Eiko Thielemann "European integration must be regarded as a crucial catalyst for the changes in domestic asylum legislation that were introduced throughout the 1990s."[34] Others like Maarten V nk instead dispute the view that the EU can exercise significant control on domestic immigration Policies. As he puts it, "that many proactive efforts to bring about a common European policy, do not necessarily imply the subsequent Europeanization of domestic politics."[35]

How has Europeanization affected Germany? Germany is one of the founding members of the European Coal and Steel Community and has been defined by many scholars as the most Europeanised EU member state. Since the end of the Second World War, Germany has always been of the most active participants in European integration and has often displayed its interest in the development of a common European immigration policy. In fact, Germany has been described as the 'front-runner' or 'motor' or 'locomotive' of European integrat on due to its strong pro-integrationalist attitude and thanks to its role in promoting supranationalism. As Alscher and Prumm put it, Germany has "been a primary actor in the process of supranational development, forcing institutional and policy transformations, always eager to erect a functioning single European market, promoting the harmonization of asylum laws."[36] An example of supranational policy-making and of Germany's preference for a communitisation of immigration policy was the amendment made to the Basic Law in 1993, which 'brought Europe in' and provided a comprehensive regulation at a European level. Some argue that since the Treaty of Amsterdam Germany has not only become less involved, but also more resistant to further integration with regards to migration pol cy. Others like Prumm and Alscher declare that "a strong limitation to German autonomy is still accepted by the German government and this position was more or less the same during the negotiations on the Amsterdam Treaty."[37] Chapter 3 will discuss the extent of Europeanization in more detail.

---

[34] Thielemann E. 'The Soft Europeanisation of Migration Policy European Integration and Domestic Policy Challenge' ECSA Seventh Biennial International Conference, May 31- June 2, 2001 p 3
[35] Vink M. 'Negative and Positive Integration in European Immigration Policies'European Integration online Papers (EIoP) Vo. 6 N. 13 August 2002 p 10
[36] Prumm K. & Alscher S. 'The Europeanization of National Policies and Politics of Immigration' in Faist T. and Ette A. 'The Europeanization of National Policies and Politics of Immigration' (New York: Palgrave Macmillan 2007) p 90
[37] Ibid p 89

Chapter 2 Immigration in Germany: A Contradictory Policy Area

This section is going to briefly analyse the historical traditions and dynamics of immigration and integration in Germany. Germany's historical legacy in immigration since the end of the Second World War has been characterised by the dictum *Deutschland ist kein Einwanderungsland*. The aim of this historical overview is to explore the reasons for the reluctance until recently of the political class to acknowledge the presence of migrants and ethnic diversity in society and to explain the contradiction between the official discourse willingly neglecting the fact that Germany is one of the main European destinations for migrants and the *de facto* immigration policies undertaken by successive governments. For this purpose, immigration policy during the Cold War era will be briefly discussed. This should help understand the various dilemmas and difficulties encountered by the Schroder government while trying to reform citizenship and transform its ethno nationalist nature.

The first wave of immigration in Germany occurred straight after the end of the Second World War when millions of ethnic Germans (*Aussiedler*) were expelled from Eastern Europe and the Soviet Union. In 1950 almost twelve million German *Vertiebene (expellees)* had entered the Federal Republic of Germany and 15.7 of West Germans were immigrants.[38] They were granted automatic German citizenship since they were considered as being part of the German 'community of descent' as a result of Article 116 of the 1949 Basic Law. The 'right to return' was thus taken advantage of by hundreds of thousands of ethnic Germans and was defined by Thranhardt "the largest single state organised migration flow in the world."[39] Albeit the considerably high inflow of migrants, the FRG endorsed further immigration to feed the hungry economy, which was recovering swiftly and therefore urgently needed to deal with the lack of manpower caused by the war. Consequently, from 1955 to 1968 the FRG singed labour recruitment agreements with the Mediterranean countries including Italy, Spain, Greece, Turkey, Portugal, Tunisia, Morocco,

---

[38] Chapin D. W. 'Germany for the Germans? The Political Effects of International Migration' (1997, Greenwood Press: Westport) p 12
[39] Thranhardt D. 'Germany's Immigration Policies and Politics' in Brochman G. And Hammar t. 'Mechanisms of Immigration control: A Comparative Analysis of European Regulation Policies' (Ocford:1999) p 36

and ex-Yugoslavia. This second wave of immigration increased the foreign population[40] from half a million to about four million- 6.5 per cent of the total population.[41] The so called 'guest workers' (*Gastarbeiter*), who were mostly employed in low-skill sectors of the economy, such as coal and iron mining or the steel and automobile industries, were considered a temporary workforce. In fact, the recruitment was based on the principle of rotation (Rotazionsprinzip) meaning that males preferably of young age would be employed to work for up to three years and would then return to their home country to be replaced by new labour. The benefits arose from not having to provide social assistance like health care or education required by permanent migration. From 1955 to 1973 eleven million out of the 14 million temporary migrants returned to their home country.[42] The large-scale recruitment of temporary migrant workers stopped in 1973 with the Oil Crisis. Industries gradually opted for long term or permanent work contracts since having to repeatedly train the new workforce was proving costly. The SPD-FDP coalition headed by Willy Brandt imposed a ban on additional recruitment (Anwerbestopp) on 23 November 1973. Simon Green notes how this measure had a dual effect: it had the "desired effect of preventing new recruitment, but it also encouraged the remaining guest workers to remain in Germany and bring their families over to join them. Ironically, [it] had the unintentional side-effect of creating a permanent immigrant minority."[43]

The FRG misjudged the situation and was slow to react since immigration did not stop but its nature did. From 1973 to 1988 the majority of the incoming immigrants was constituted by family members of guest workers, increasing the total foreign population from four million to 4.8 million.[44] The government failed to take measures fostering social and political integration of immigrants and preferred to stay in a state of denial vis-a-vis the growing presence of permanent minority communities. Very little effort was made to integrate the guest workers and their families, which were not viewed as permanent members of society. As von Stritzky put it, "immigrants often lived in poor neighbourhoods, where they created their own subcultures over the years. The educational success of the second generation was

---

[40] **Note**- Excluding the number of ethnic Germans since they were granted citizenship and considered German
[41] Chapin D. W 1997
[42] Green S, 'Immigration, asylum and citizenship in Germany: The impact of unification and the Berlin republic,' *West European Politics*, Vo. 29 No. 1, 1 October 2001 pp 87
[43] Ibid p 88
[44] Chapin D. W 1997 p

limited, access to work was difficult and naturalisation policies restrictive."[45] Layton-Henry highlights the importance of integrating *Gastarbeiter* family members "once family reunification takes place and migrant communities become established, then access to social and political rights becomes much more important."[46] The government eventually formed a broader policy framework in 1977, but the report for the Advancement of the Integration of Foreign Workers and their Families primarily recommended encouraging foreign workers to head back to their native country.[47]

A fourth source of immigration in the late 1980s was represented by an extremely large number of asylum-seekers, who took advantage of the generous social and financial benefits guaranteed by Article 16 of the Basic Law. Indeed the law recognised "the right of asylum-seekers to make an application rather then- as in other countries- the responsibility of the state to consider a claim."[48]

From 1977 to 2003, Germany received almost three million applications for asylum. Only in 1992, eighty per cent of asylum applications in Western Europe (almost 500 000) were made in Germany.[49] If on the one side the government was constrained by its 'special obligation's after the Second World War, on the other pressure for changing the law came from the Lander, the economic burden of reunification and the rapidly growing support for the extreme right-wing parties like the NDP and the Republikaner due to exceptionally high levels of unemployment combined to the rising racist sentiments among the population. As a result, the amendment to Article 16 was made by the Asylum Compromise of 1993, which aligned Germany with other EU member states and the 1990 Dublin Convention. The legal reforms through EU co-operation policy on asylum were proved successful for the number of applicants fell dramatically. For instance, in 2006 only 21 000 applications were made, the lowest level since 1983.[50]

---

[45] Von Stritzky J. 'Germany's Immigration Policy: From Refusal to Reluctance' *ARI* 93 3/6/2009 p 2
[46] Layton-Henry Z. 'Citizenship and Migrant Workers in Western Europe' in Vogel U. & Moran M. 'The Frontiers of Citizenship' (Houndmills: Macmillan, 1991) p 114
[47] Green S. 2001 p 87
[48] Geddes A. 'The Politics of Migration and Immigration in Europe' (London,Sage Publications: 2003) p 85
[49] Ibid
[50] Von Stritzky J. 2009 p 2

However, if these legal reforms helped reduce asylum immigration, yet the overall amount of immigrants did not sink. Towards the end of 2002, 7.3 million foreigners were living in Germany with an increase of over one-third since German reunification. Over nine per cent of the population was composed by non-nationals, the highest level in the European Union, and it included two million Turks, two million EU nationals, and one million people from ex-Yugoslavia. [51] Over twenty nations have at least fifty thousand representatives with a permanent resident in Germany, which is therefore a country with an extremely large and diverse foreign population of various types.[52] This represents a considerable social and political challenge for a country with a brief colonial past and once known as country of emigration rather than immigration. Moreover, this shows how Germany has undergone a noticeable cultural diversification of its immigrant population. The Turkish community remains the main immigrant group, but the number of foreigners from different parts of the world settling in Germany is increasing year by year. The amount of foreign seasonal workers from the member states of the European Union, especially Ireland, Portugal, Poland and several Eastern European countries, has increased steadily in the last two decades.[53] Many of them constitute the temporary or transitory low-cost workforce in the construction industry or in economic activities such as taxi drivers, cleaning or agricultural assistance.

In the light of these realities, why has the official political discourse in Germany been reluctant until recently to acknowledge the presence of migrants and ethnic diversity in society? Even though it is apparent that the sentence –'Germany is not an immigration country'– completely fails to depict the social reality, many mainstream politicians, the more conservative in particular, have continued to utter the slogan during political elections and debates. The statement was repeated 158 times during the election campaign in 1998![54] Until the 1980s, one of the main arguments put forward by several governments was that since Germany was not actively seeking new permanent immigration, there was no need to undertake substantial formal policies common in other EU countries where immigration had instead been acknowledged. Thus, the integration of immigrants was not deemed as necessary since immigrants were still viewed as temporary 'guests.' Even after the only significant policy

---

[51] Green S. 2004, p 7
[52] Ibid
[53] Von Stritzky 2009 p 3
[54] Drieschner F. 'Ist Multikulti schuld?' Die Zeit nr 16 , 12/04/2006 http://www.zeit.de/2006/16/contra Accessed on 28/08/09

characterised by the formulation of the Guidelines on Naturalization in 1977 (Einburgerungsrichtlinien), which rejected dual citizenship, the denial of being a country of immigration remained. The contradiction between the official discourse willingly neglecting the fact that Germany is one of the main European destinations for migrants and the *de facto* immigration policies undertaken by successive governments can be explained by several factors.

First, this stance was the as a result of the 'policy of dissuasion' – *Abschreckungspolitik*.[55] According to this doctrine, any official recognition or acknowledgment of immigration in Germany risks reinforcing migratory dynamics. Secondly, politicians are also aware of the widespread anti-migration sentiment shared by a noticeable portion of society. Feminist leader Alice Schwarzer once stated that "after the Nazis condemned everything foreign, their children now want to love everything foreign, with their eyes closed tightly."[56] This assertion appeared to be in contrast with the view of the majority of the population. As a speaker of the Humanist Union pointed out, the Kein Einwanderungsland claim "is a crude lie but it does capture the attitude and opinions of many people who do not want to accept certain changes in society, or who would even like to reverse them."[57] As we have seen, the growing anti-immigrant sentiment due to the fear of *Uberfremdung* ('excessive immigration by alien cultures') manifested in racist attacks in Rostock and in the rise of extreme right-wing parties, were one of the main factors pushing the government to amend policy on asylum. Finally, and most importantly, this obstination can be partly explained by the traditional ethnocultural model of German nationhood, which made German citizenship culturally and ethnically exclusive thereby impeding a significant amount of naturalisations of immigrants. This can be best summarised by the words pronounced in the 1980s by professor Kay Hailbronner, currently working for the BAMF (*Bundesamt für Migration und Flüchtlinge*): "conceiving of the Federal Republic as a country of immigration with multiple national minorities would contradict the Basic Law's conception of a provisional state geared toward the recovery of national unity."[58]

---

[55] See Vogel, Dita: 2000, 'Migration control in Germany and the United States' *International Migration Review* Vo. 34, No. 2, 390-422
[56] Quoted in Dregger Alfred quoted in Carle R. 'Citizenship Debates in the New Germany' *Springer Science* Vo. 44 August 2007 p 149
[57] Quoted in Klopp Brett 2002 p 10
[58] Cited in Joppke C. 'Immigration and the Nation-State' (Oxford, 1999: Oxford University Press) p 63

The Schroder government attempted to change the ethnocultural model and its exclusive definitions of citizenship and nationality by crafting new policies and replacing the 1913 citizenship law, which remained in power until 1999 and made naturalisation for non-ethnic Germans extremely complicated.' The red-green coalition realised that the notion that Germany is not a country of immigration was creating a contradictory policy framework, under which confusing laws and regulations were being stipulated with the effect of marginalising its large immigrant population. The ethnocultural notion of citizenship and nationality was an obstacle to the integration of the large immigrant population because it still prevented the naturalisation of immigrants, thereby excluding them from the political community. As the Federal Constitutional Court stated a decade ago, "the only possible approach to solving the gap between the permanent population and democratic participation lies in changing the nationality law by facilitating the acquisition of the German nationality by foreigners living permanently in Germany."[59] Therefore, the next section is going to analyse some of the main policy reforms on citizenship undertaken by the Schroder administration, which liberalised the 1913 law and openly questioned the 'no country of immigration' formula causing it to recede from public debates.

---

[59] Baubock R. Groenendijk K. Waldrauch H. 'Acquisition and Loss of Nationality' (2006 Amsterdam: Amsterdam University Press) p 220

Chapter 3 Citizenship and Integration in Germany

If the infamous *Kein Einwanderungs Land* assumption has been left behind, has the integration of the foreign population become easier? Has the naturalization of immigrants, especially from the Turkish community, become less difficult and has the perceived division between 'us' and 'them' been reduced? Is there still a contrast between the treatment reserved to the Turkish community and that held in reserve to the ethnic Germans, and if so, is it linked to the different notions of assimilation and integration? This chapter is going to test the hypothesis that immigrants are still expected to assimilate rather than integrate.

3.1 The 2000 Nationality Act

In 2001 Roger Brubaker described the German citizenship policy as an "egalitarian apartheid, an institutionalized separateness, suggested in the oxymoronic phrase *unsere auslandische Mitburger* – our foreign fellow citizens."[60] Whilst the provocative statement does arguably present a degree of truth, the 2000 Nationality Act represents a major first step towards a more pluralistic view of the concept of citizenship and has considerably facilitated the previously arduous task of becoming a German citizen. As Frank Eckardt declared, "for the first time in German history the immigrants' right to integration is recognized."[61]

Right after the historic election win in September 1998, Schroder's coalition worked on an ambitious law proposal with the objective of facilitating the naturalisation process for foreigners by introducing the principle of *ius soli* and, most controversially, dual citizenship for foreign children born and raised in Germany. In a memorable speech to the Bundestag two months after his appointment as Chancellor, Schroder motivated his ambitious plan to reform the citizenship law:

---

[60] Brubaker R. ;The return to assimilation? Changing perspectives on immigration and its sequels in France, Germany, and the United States' *Ethnic and Racial Studies* Vo. 24 N. 4 July 2001p 538
[61] Eckardt F. 2007 p237

"For far too long those who have come to work here, who pay their taxes and abide by our laws have been told they are just 'guests'. But in truth they have for years been part of German society. The government will modernise the law on nationality. That will enable those living permanently in Germany and their children born here to acquire full rights of citizenship. No one who wants to be a German citizen should have to renounce or deny his foreign roots. That is why we will also allow dual nationality. This is responding positively to the realities in Europe. Our national consciousness depends not on some law of descent of Wilhelmine tradition but on the self-assured democracy we now have."[62]

Schroder's words clearly highlighted the strong determination and the high expectations embedded in the law proposal. However, the CDU/CSU counterpart, who defined citizenship in ethno nationalist terms, fiercely opposed the proposal of dual citizenship because in their view it would not encourage integration, but instead persuade the 'new' citizens to have divided loyalties. Wolfgang Schauble, at that time head of the CDU, argued that "regularly allowing dual citizenship is poison to integration as well as to domestic order."[63] The intense political debates that followed ignited the anti-immigrant sentiment of public opinion and the centre-right coalition decided to ride the wave by taking the debates to the streets and calling for a national plebiscite on dual citizenship right before the upcoming regional elections to the state parliament in Hessen, the region surrounding Frankfurt, in February 1999. The petition against dual citizenship incredibly received more than five million signatures and the whole campaign of the CDU in Hessen focused on the opposition to the proposed citizenship reform.[64] As a matter of fact, public surveys showed that over sixty three per cent of Germans were against the reform.[65] Consequently, due to the exceptional public mobilization organized mainly by Edmund Stoiber, the arch conservative Bavarian chairman of the CSU, the SPD/Green government faced a striking defeat in what had traditionally been the stronghold of the Social Democrats since 1945. The SPD-Green coalition lost the majority of the seats in the Bundesrat, the upper house of parliament, and

---

[62] Gerhard Schroder speech 10 November 1998 *German Information Center* http://www.germany.info/relaunch/politics/speeches/111098.html. Accessed on 20/08/09

[63] Birnbaum R. 'Schauble : Doppelte Staatsburgerschaft ist Gift fur Die Integration' *Der Tagespiel* 4 January 1999

[64] Hansen R. & Koehler J. 'Issue Definition, Political Discourse and the Politics of Nationality Reform in France and Germany' European Journal of Political Research 44/5 (2005) p 638

[65] Ibid

the CDU/CSU were thus able to veto any legislation. As a result, the government's original proposal was modified through the introduction of restrictive measures.

Following intense parliamentary debates in March and May 1999, the *Bundesrat* eventually passed the new reformed citizenship law, which came into force on 1 January 2000 and was defined by many political analysts as a 'messy political compromise' between the main political parties.[66] Nevertheless, the SPD/Green Party coalition crafted a policy which made naturalisation easier by granting the possibility, for the first time, to non-ethnic Germans and children born in the country to acquire German citizenship. *Ius soli* was in fact introduced for the first time in German history. Even though the Germany Nationality Act of 2000 had been modified, nonetheless it undoubtedly represented an unprecedented and unique move towards a more pluralistic view of the concept of citizenship. The new spirit of the law and its intent to eradicate the traditional concept of nation became apparent when the minister of the interior Otto Schily, one of the main promoters of the reform, stated: "It is very interesting to remember what the French philosopher Ernest Renan had to say...about what constitutes a nation. He looked into the question whether a nation is constituted by an ethnie and concluded that this could not be true. The Germans have Celtic, Slavic and Germanic origins and is a total ethnic mix which one cannot decipher anymore."[67] Initially, this historic reform produced some positive outcomes. In 2000, the number of naturalisations rose sharply reaching the total figure of almost 200 000. However, in the following years, the amount of foreign residents opting for naturalisation have gradually decreased each year until 2007, when only 113 000 acquired German citizenship.[68] These disappointing figures are the result of the many flaws enclosed in the new citizenship law. For instance, the path to naturalisation appears to be filled with a high number of obstacles, given the presence of various conditions and requirements which seem exceedingly demanding in the eyes of many in the foreign communities. Adults are subject to challenging language and civic tests, even more difficult for the members of the former *Gastarbeiter*, who had rarely put any effort into learning German given the fact that

---

[66] Hansen R. & Koehler J. 'Issue Definition, Political Discourse and the Politics of Nationality Reform in France and Germany' European Journal of Political Research 44/5 (2005) p 638

[67] Otto Schily cited in Heckmann Friedrich 'From Ethnic Nation to Universalistic Immigrant Integration: Germany' edited by Heckman =n F. & Schnapper D. 'The integration of immigrants in European societies' EFMS (2003, Lucius: Stuttgart) p 59

[68] Statistisches Bundesamt Deutschland 'Foreign population' 2009

they were expected to eventually return to their home countries. Moreover, the tests are administered by the Lander and, consequently, their reliability appeared questionable. As Professor Holly Hansen-Thomas noted, "*Because* some states are more conservative, while others are more liberal, their implementation of the test can reflect the prevailing ideologies on naturalisation."[69] In addition, the application fees for naturalisation are extremely costly, the adult applicants are required to have a valid residence permit, a profitable employment, no criminal convictions, express commitment to the Basic Law and, most importantly, they need to renounce their nationality. Thus, even though Claudia Roth, the chairman of the Green Party, perhaps exaggerated when she declared that 'for many foreigners concerned, the laws have worsened their living conditions,'[70] naturalization is still difficult to achieve.

For children born and raised in Germany with immigrant parents, it is a different matter because via the 'option-model' *(Optionsmodell)* they are granted a dual citizenship until the age of 23, age after which they must chose one or the other citizenship. However, children born to foreign parents are allowed to acquire German citizenship through *ius soli* only if their parents have lived in the country for a minimum of eight years combined to a corresponding residence permit. Thus, in practice, only about half of the children qualify for the *ius soli,* for the amount of foreigners who have lived for at least eight years in Germany is significantly higher than that of the non-nationals with the necessary residence permit. The restriction in fact precludes the acquirement of German citizenship for about sixty per cent of the children born in Germany since the law has been put into effect.[71]

In addition, a majority of German-born children with immigrant parents find themselves in a dilemma and experience an identity conflict since, on the one hand, they are required to embrace the German cultural tradition and, on the other, are encouraged by their families to maintain their native identity. Hansen-Thomas argues that this problematic situation affects the Turkish children the strongest because "not only must they fit into German social, political, educational, and civic categories of identity, but they must also be able to interact within identities as dictated by their family, which can include religious, language-

---

[69] Hansen-Thomas H. 'Language ideology, citizenship, and identity: The case of modern Germany' *Journal of Language and Politics* 6:2 (2007) p259

[70] Cited in Eckardt F. 2007 p241

[71] Howard M.M. 'The Causes and Consequences of Germany's New Citizenship Law' *German Politics* Vo. 17 No. 1 March 2008 p 53

based, and cultural."⁷² For the Aussiedlers, the process was considerably simpler because they were not expected to renounce their Polish or Russian citizenship, for this was viewed as being an 'unreasonable hardship' (*Unzumutbare Harte*). Thus, the technical and legal deficits of the citizenship reform combined with the double standard reserved to the ethnic Germans highlight how the German understanding of citizenship was exclusive. The introduction of double nationality was expected to "introduce a general shift in integration policies towards a multicultural approach that redefines the basis of German nationality."⁷³ Yet, as Green notes, "if the introduction of *ius soli* constitutes the main innovation of the new law, it is the steadfast desire to avoid dual citizenships which lies at the heart of Germany's citizenship policy."⁷⁴ The prohibition of dual citizenship makes the liberalisation process incomplete, especially if compared to Schroder's initial high ambitions. But why was it so difficult for the government to introduce amendments and for what reasons did German conservatives view dual citizenship as 'poison' to integration? The next section is going to attempt to find some of the possible explanations by analyzing the famous political debate on culture and nationality which followed the introduction of the 2000 Nationality Act.

3.2 The Leitkultur Debate: Assimilation or Integration?

Following the incomplete citizenship reform, the Interior Minister Otto Schily recruited a team of experts to advise the government on immigration policy. The Sussmuth Commission, named after its chairwoman, was set up in July 2000 and was constituted by various politicians, academics, religious leaders and representatives of business and interest groups. The main objective was to set down a new set of proposals for immigration, integration and citizenship.⁷⁵ The Commission published its results in July 2001 and stated that 'Germany needs immigrants' and that better coexistence between Germans and immigrants via integration were essential. Moreover, the government was advised to "open

---

⁷² Howard M.M. 'The Causes and Consequences of Germany's New Citizenship Law' German Politics Vo. 17 No. 1 March 2008 p 261
⁷³ Eckardt F. 2007 p 242
⁷⁴ Green S. 'Beyond ethnoculturalsim? German citizenship in the new millenium' *German Politics* 9:3 2000 p 116
⁷⁵ Padgett S.; Paterson W.E.; Smith G. 2003 p 242

up to entrepreneurs and highly qualified workers" as well as "implementing a comprehensive integration programme."[76] These affirmations prompted great irritation among the CDU and CSU politicians, who accused the centre-left of 'jeopardising German cultural identity.' In autumn 2000, a conservative representative of the CDU/CSU, Friedrich Merz, affirmed that non-national immigrants should be induced to adopt Germany 's 'dominant culture' (*Leitkultur*) and thereby set off a heated intellectual debate over what it meant to be German. The *Leitkultur*'s concept of culture was based on the belief that the nation is a 'fatherland' offering a community with a shared destiny, language, culture, and identity, which provide a political and cultural framework.[77] The importance of placing the nation at the centre of political thinking is explained by Alfred Mechtersheimer, a political scientist and former member of parliament:

"National refers to the nation, that is to say to a community based on a political act of will by people who are laying claim not just to a shared identity but also to their right to be different. What a people have in common may be culture, language, religion or history; the nation manifests itself in a political consciousness of common values, intensions and a wish to prevail...it is clear that the nation satisfies in a particularly profound way the basic social need of people for a sense of belonging."[78]

This emphasis on culture, the 'Volk' (the people) and the nation has been viewed by many as going hand in hand with racist attitudes, since the *Leitkulturdebatte* essentially replaces the notion of race with that of culture with the transformation of ius sanguinis into what could be defined as 'ius cultus.'[79] Different cultures cannot coexist and should remain separate in order to avoid conflicts. 'Prussian values' (order, discipline, punctuality, a sense of duty, and physical toughness) are constantly threatened by the foreign population. Multiculturalism is thus viewed as a form of disintegration causing society to fall apart into a plurality of ways of life and, thus, ethnocultural homogeneity of the Europeans should be encouraged. As a result, ethnic minorities should assimilate to German culture. Indeed, the CDU/CSU proposed guidelines for new immigration policies involved the embracing of the

---

[76] Cited in Kruse I; Orren E.H. ;Angenendt S December 2003 p 131
[77] Woods Roger (2007) p 96
[78] Mechtersheimer A. quoted in Woods R. 'Germany's New Right as culture and politics'(2007,London: Palgrave Macmillan)p 37-38
[79] Ibid

Leitkultur, which must require "more than just acquisition of the language and the recognition of laws', for it included "tolerance and consideration for the norms and customs" of the indigenous population...rooted in Christianity, the enlightenment and humanism."[80] Many conservative thinkers point out that even the constitution of the German Republic is based on the belief that the modern German state is founded on 'one culture and one nation.' According to Merz, the predominant culture has "its foundation in the Constitution as the most important expression of German moral order guaranteeing the coherence of German society."[81]

The Leitkulturdebatte was not unique in its kind as it was preceded by several attempts by CDU and CSU members to start a debate about national consciousness and the integration of immigrants. For instance, Jorg Schonbohm, right-wing CDU politician and former home secretary for Brandenburg, argued that to become a member of the German Staatsvolk, "immigrants have to aspire to its culture, which has developed since Otto the Great, wholeheartedly, and not just because of the personal benefits of immigration."[82] Thus, a degree of assimilation is essential to avoid conflict between parallel societies. Foreigners have to accept "the basic habits and customs of the German population...there is no space for the political conflicts of foreign countries on German soil."[83] Many CDU representatives like Alfred Dregger opposed the concept of multiculturalism, on the grounds that "every state has to serve its own citizens first, and only secondarily the rest of the world" because Germany "cannot become everyone's country."[84] Perhaps the most eloquent statement summarizing and highlighting the adversity to multiculturalism was made by the Interior Minister of the Kohl administration, who formulated a draft affirming that "the self-understanding of the Federal Republic of Germany as a German state is at stake...The FRG would develop into a multinational and multicultural society, which would be permanently plagued by minority problems...the national interest commands us to stop such a

---

[80] CSU 'Zehn Leitlinien fur eine gesetzliche Regelung zur Zuwanderung' (2000) http://www.csu.de Accessed on 15/08/09
[81] Pautz H. 'The politics of identity in Germany : the *Leitkultur* debate' *Race and Class* Vo. 46 N. 4, 2005 p 45
[82] Schonbohm J. *Junge Freiheit* (19 March 1997)
[83] Schonbohm J. *Berliner Morgenpost* (24 April 1997)
[84] Dregger Alfred quoted in Carle R. 2007 p 147

development in its very beginning....Germany's common history, heritage, language, and culture would lose their unifying and defining nature."[85]

These notions of nationhood and citizenship were fundamental in shaping immigration policies in the last decade. Nationhood, as Brubaker explains, was visualized not as the holder of universal political values, but as an "organic cultural linguistic community; the nationhood is constituted by ethnocultural unity."[86] Citizenship is therefore conceived as more than just a type of membership. The Green party and the SPD argued against the Wilhelmian notions of citizenship and supported a multicultural society which "confirms the cultural freedom of the individual allows for differentiation and dissociates itself from the idea of a German Leitkultur aiming at assimilation and subordination." [87] The progressive left moved the focus away from the concept of nation-state, described by some as 'a disaster for Europe.' In fact, according to the Green Party the idea of a multicultural society is not centred on the concept of nation-state, but 'on the indivisibility of human rights.' Thus, "citizenship should not determine the rights of the individual, but where an individual lives."[88] They viewed multiculturalism as a way of creating a new world order based on social harmony, the defence of minority rights, and cosmopolitanism. The multicultural model favours integration over assimilation, regarded as 'forced Germanisation' (Zwagsgermanisierung) and an attack on the ethnic identities of immigrants. Integration, instead, unites together different social groups and reduces conflicts amongst them to the minimum.

However, as we have seen with the elections in Hesse, the majority of the German population dislikes this multicultural model and shares the conservative view that integration equals assimilation. This view is spreading even more because the Turkish community in Germany, which is the country's largest ethnic minority with its 2.6 million units, is forming a 'state within a state.' More than 200,000 residents, forty five per cent of children under the age of 16 have a migration background, which means that they are

---

[85] Joppke C. 'Multiculturalism and Immigration' *Theory and Society* 25, 1996 p471
[86] Brubaker W.R 1992 p 17
[87] 'Kruse I; Orren E.H. ;Angenendt S. 'The failure of immigration reform in Germany' *German Politics* 1 December 2003 p 142
[88] Joppke C. 'Selecting By Origin' (Cambridge: Harvard University Press, 2005) p 466

immigrants themselves or have parents or grandparents who immigrated into the country.[89] Across Germany itself, the proportion is of almost a third. Stolz and Krebs argue that there is a risk that this large ethnic minority might create 'parallel societies' unable to coexist with German culture and values and give birth to forms of transnational communities with economic, social, political and cultural legacies in both Germany and their home countries. Turkey's prime minister, Recep Tayyip Erdogan, further exacerbated this widespread fear among the German population when, on a official visit to Germany in February 2008, urged the Turkish community to hold itself detached from German society since "assimilation is a crime against humanity...and Turkish children should be able to study in Turkish language schools and at a Turkish university."[90] Many Turks living in Germany, on the other hand, argue that the indigenous population does not facilitate the process of integration since however high they rise and however good their German is, they continue to be considered foreign. Indeed, according to a study conducted by Faruk Yen of the Centre for Studies on Turkey in Essen, over two-thirds of Turkish residents consider themselves as victims of discrimination.[91] According to statistics provided by the Ministry of Labour, only 33.6 per cent of foreign respondents affirmed that they 'felt rooted in Germany' and only 48 per cent indicated that they 'felt comfortable living in Germany.[92] Statements such as that made by the former Chancellor Helmut Kohl during a debate on citizenship reform, which expressed the view that "if we were to yield on the question of double citizenship, then in a short time we would have not three million, but four, five or six million Turks in our land,"[93] only deepen concerns. It is also noteworthy to draw attention to the fact that a particularly high number of former *gastarbeiter* continue to view themselves not as permanent residents, but as a temporary workforce, and consequently seek not to achieve greater integration, even after forty years spent in Germany. As Annette Treibel explains, "The goal of guest workers was not to create a new life for themselves in the host country, but instead to make possible an existence for themselves and their families in the homeland."[94] Thus,

---

[89] 'Two unamalgamated worlds', The Economist April 5th 2008 p 31
[90] Ibid
[91] Ibid
[92] Cited in Doerschler P. 'Push-Pull Factors and Immigrant Political Integration in Germany' *Social Science Quarterly* Vo. 87 No. 5 December 2006 p 1103
[93] Checkel T.J '(Regional) Norms and (Domestic) Social Mobilization: Citizenship Politics in Post-Maastricht, Post-Cold War Germany'*Arena Working* Papers 99/3 February 1999 p 3
[94] Treibel Annette cited in Doerschler 2006 p 1103

immigrants that are motivated by economic reasons are more likely to focus on material gains and are often disinterested in the politics of the host country. As Peter Doerschler puts it, "few economic immigrants in Germany have had an incentive to deepen aspects of their social and political integration, such as learning German, developing personal relationships with natives, or becoming more engaged in German politics" because doing so would redirect resources and time away from the primary and most important economic goal.[95]

Nevertheless, this feeling of exclusion is exacerbated by the contrast between the treatment reserved to the Turkish community and that held in reserve to the ethnic Germans. Approximately two and a half million Aussiedler entered Germany between 1990 and 2002. They were granted German citizenship which allowed them to benefit from civic, political and social rights without at first having to contribute to the social security system. While the Turkish community was negatively affected by the *ius sanguinis* principle, the ethnic Germans were regarded as a cultural part of the national community. Christian Jopke points out that "What has started as a temporary measure to integrate the millions of ethnic Germans who were actually expelled from their homeland after World War II was expanded...into an open-door policy for anyone from a communist country who could claim, however remotely, German origin."[96] The *Aussiedlers* were entitled to the same benefits, such as access to health insurance or unemployment and pension benefits, as other Germans. As Geddes puts it, the *Aussiedler* were treated as though they had lived in Germany for their whole lives."[97] However, the integration of the ethnic Germans, one of the main sources of immigration to Germany, has been problematic for several reasons. Despite them being automatically awarded citizenship, ethnic Germans have been facing challenges similar to those of the non-nationals. For instance, their proficiency in German and their knowledge of German culture is often considerably low. Additionally, many ethnic Germans find it difficult to enter the labour market due to the fact that their qualifications obtained in their former host country are seldom recognized in Germany and also because their skills are not required. Thus, as Marc Morje Howard points out, "the striking contrast between German-born Turks (speaking fluent German, often studying and working productively in Germany) and the large numbers of ethnic Germans is becoming more and

---

[95] Treibel Annette cited in Doerschler 2006 p 1103
[96] Joppke 2005 p 174
[97] Geddes A. 2003 p 92

more difficult to sustain."[98] Even though since the 1990s there have been increasing restrictions and Aussiedler are slowly starting to be treated like the rest of the German migrant population, with a move from a 'community of belonging' to a 'community of contributors to the GNP'[99], nevertheless the disparity of treatment between the two migrant groups symbolizes even now the strength of the ethnographic notion of citizenship and identity. The next section is going to explore some of the factors that could force Germany to move towards a more inclusive society based on a civic model of citizenship.

---

[98] Howard M.M. 2008 p43
[99] See Bommes M. & Geddes A. 'Immigration and Welfare: Challenging the Borders of the Welfare State (London: Routledge, 2000)

Chapter 4 The Impact of Domestic and External pressure

There are a myriad of factors shaping domestic politics and dynamics. Some of them have a more significant impact than others in acting as a form of pressure on governments to liberalise, modernize, and take a less restrictive approach to immigration and integration policy. This section is going to analyse perhaps the most pressing issues, which may affect policy-making more than others, namely the demographic and skill shortages on the one side, and the European Union on the other. Of course, countless other endogenous as well as exogenous factors play an important role. The regional elections in Hessen emphasized the crucial role of the sixteen *Lander*, which have the power to use their constitutional right to limit the central government's power. The federal states have the ability to act directly in the policy making process through the *Bundesrat*, the upper chamber of the parliament, through which they are able to veto any bill sponsored by the central government and can therefore "exercise an important collective check on the federal government's scope for action."[100] The terrorist attacks on 11 September 2001 have also severely affected policy-making on immigration by inducing Western governments to take a more restrictive and stringent approach. However, these are examples of endogenous and exogenous factors that were central in slowing down the process of policy modernization and liberalization. Instead, the interest of this study is to assess the role of the European Union and the demographic/skill shortages in acting as a dynamic force towards changing domestic policy-making on immigration and national conceptions of citizenship and identity. To what extent can these factors push Germany towards a civic model? Would the liberalizing changes to the concept of citizenship be occurring in any case, even without the Europeanization process or the domestic pressures?

---

[100] Green 2004 p 12

4.1 Demographic and Labour Shortage

Germany is currently facing a severe demographic shortage. In 2004, Germany's fertility rate was just over one child per woman, nowhere near the 2.2 level required for the stability of the population.[101]. Germany has one of the lowest percentages of children citizens in the world and around forty-five per cent of Germans claimed to prefer to be childless.[102] Unsurprisingly, Chemnitz is believed to have the lowest birth rate in the world. In addition, life expectancy has gone up and at the beginning of the new century it was positioned at 75 for men and 81 for women.[103] The German social system will risk falling into crisis due to the high number of pensioners combined with the low percentage of workers, indispensable for a well functioning tax system. If birth rates continue to fall, there will be a smaller workforce to support the older generations. Even with a yearly immigration of 200,000 people, its population is expected to fall from the current 83 million to about 73 million by 2050.[104] Historian Gerhard Hirschfield affirmed that a rate of about 350,000 immigrants will be required in order to maintain the current standard of living.[105] Of course, immigration alone cannot solve the problem of low birth rates. For instance, according to the Office for National Statistics, Britain's population in 2008 reached 61.4 million and received the biggest increase in a single year since 1962 as a result not of immigration but of the nation's astoundingly high fertility rate, which reached its highest level for 15 years.[106] Germany has a dwindling birth rate due to several factors that range from poor child care and inflexible labour laws to high youth unemployment and extended higher education. Consequently, the Merkel administration has recently pushed Germany's declining birth rate to the top of the political agenda and has introduced a number of proposals to persuade more couples to have children. Some of them involve a 'state-funded child welfare support' that will allow parents to receive 67 per cent of their previous incomes while staying at home for up to 12 months, as well as compensation for up to 4000 Euros of childcare costs each year.[107] The

---

[101] Green S. 'Divergent Traditions, Converging Responses: Immigration and Integration Policy in the UK and Germany', *German Politics* 16/1 2007 p101- 102
[102] Carle R 2007 p152
[103] Ibid
[104] Ibid
[105] Ibid p 154
[106] Savage M. 'Baby boom drives British population to record high' *The Independent* 28 August 2009
[107] BBC News 'Dwindling Germans review policies' March 2006
http://news.bbc.co.uk/1/hi/world/europe/4852040.stm Accessed on 28/08/09

long term effectiveness of these schemes remains to be seen. Until then, recruiting new labour migrants, but also facilitating naturalisation and the integration process of the foreign children born in Germany through the introduction of double nationality would be undoubtedly a helpful way of improving the grim figures.

The evident skill shortages in crucial areas of the economy are a considerable challenge associated with demographic decline. Even though levels of unemployment are considerably high, surveys have demonstrated that there is a consistent lack of skilled labour in specific sectors of the economy like engineering or pharmaceutics.[108] German interests groups and industries warned of the inevitable negative impact on the economy of the labour shortage in both the low skilled and the high skilled area, insisting that a corresponding recruitment of foreign works was an urgent necessity. As Merih Anil makes clear, "liberalising citizenship regulation was also seen as a way to improve Germany's image in order to attract highly skilled workers...compared to traditional immigrant-receiving countries, Germany's exclusive citizenship policy was a disadvantage in the highly competitive international labour market for skilled workers."[109] The acute skill shortages manifested when the SPD-Green coalition implemented the Green Card programme in 2000 with the intent to attract IT experts from abroad. In fact, the German labour market was unable to offer a skilled workforce in this sector albeit the high levels of unemployment (4 million)[110]. The scheme intended to give out residence and work permits for 5 years to up to twenty thousand third-country nationals. Between 2000 and 2003, the government received less than 15,000 applications mainly from India and Eastern Europe.[111] The highly competitive nature of the international labour markets in a globalised economy and the better offers (for instance, permanent residence permits) made by other Western countries such as the US contributed to the poor results of the Green Card programme, which was put to a stop in 2004. Nevertheless, the initiative had a symbolic effect on the debate on immigration and integration. As Green put it, "with labour shortages in key sectors increasing, and with the United Nations calculating that Germany requires 458,000 immigrants annually just to stabilise the size of its working population, the agenda has switched from preventing

---

[108] Green S. 2007 p103
[109] Anil M 'No More Foreigners? The remaking of German Naturalization and Citizenship Law, 1990-200' *Dialectical Anthropology* 29/ 3-4 2005 p 460.
[110] Von Stritzky Johannes 2009 p 4
[111] Ibid

immigration to managing labour migration."[112] The question was not if Germany needed immigration but how much. In fact, the Green Card initiative was justified by the Sussmuth Commission set up shortly afterwards. As we have seen in the previous chapter, the commission not only claimed that Germany needs immigrants, but argued in favour of a more comprehensive integration programme. The advice of the commission was then strongly criticised by the conservatives and was followed by the Leitkultur debate. However, the fact that the government has moved from preventing immigration to managing labour migration can be considered as a premonitory sign that the ethnographic notions of citizenship and nationality will eventually come under increasing pressure in a globalised economy with a highly competitive international labour market. As Thranhardt observed, industrialists started to "oscillate between their conservative leanings, ideas that immigration is an economic necessity in time of demographic change, and an interest in cheap and motivated labour force.'"[113]

4.2 Europeanization of Immigration Policy and Identity?

Another factor shaping the government policies is the European Union. Over the last fifteen years, its major bodies - the Council of Europe, the European Commission, the European Court of Justice, and the European Court of Human Rights- have undoubtedly strengthened their political, moral, and judicial role, thereby affecting to some extent German policy making. There have been significant changes since the end of the Cold War. Transformations at a European level can transform the 'nature of the political climate within which issues have to be dealt with at the national level.'[114] The first move towards change was made with the stipulation of the Treaty on European Union in Maastricht in 1992 and in many respects it represented a key historical moment. For instance, for the first time in history a European Union citizenship was established, thereby weakening the exclusivity of national citizenship. As Dora Kostakopoulou puts it, European citizenship was based on the already existing Community law rights of free movement and residence and, "with the exception of electoral

---
[112] Green S.2001 p 100
[113] Thranhardt D. 'Germany's Immigration Policies and Politics' in Brochman G. And Hammar t. 'Mechanisms of Immigration control: A Comparative Analysis of European Regulation Policies' (Ocford:1999) p 35
[114] Day S. 'Dealing with Alien Suffrage: Ecamples from the EU and Germany' *Centre for the Study of Law in Europe* 22 May 2000 p 3

rights at local and European Parliament, it did not add much new to existing Community Law."[115] Moreover, the Union citizenship was initially meant to complement and not replace national citizenship and was thus considered a vague concept. However as the Commission declared in a report in 2001, European Union citizenship is "both a source of legitimation of the process of European integration, by reinforcing the participation of citizens, and a fundamental factor in the creation among citizens of a sense of belonging to the European Union and having a genuine European identity."[116] Hence, it is a first –albeit small- step towards the replacement of the nationality model, especially the one based on a homogeneous ethnocultural community, with a more inclusive conception of citizenship. Of course, it is true to say that the Europeanization of nationality or citizenship is at most still evolving and hesitant considering that each individual stat still applies its own domestic policies regarding permanent residence or naturalisation. Thus, the amount of convergence appears much lower in citizenship and integration policy than in other areas such as the single market. Even if European citizenship is being gradually transformed 'from above,' this has not cancelled the concept of national citizenship of individual member states. The German government has often shown resistance to any attempt to make changes to the character of EU citizenship established by the Maastricht Treaty.

Nevertheless, the European Union has continuously attempted to strengthen its role in setting goals for common policies in order to create a distinct European politics of immigration, as demonstrated by the Amsterdam Treaty in 1997 whereby immigration policy has evolved from a 'loose intergovernmental cooperation to a partially communitarised policy-making area.'[117] Immigration is affecting the whole of Western Europe and, albeit immigration being a 'high politics' area with the consequent refusal of most states to give away sovereignty, most members of the EU including Germany have demonstrated to favour cooperation though institutions in order to find common solutions. Immigration and asylum have been incorporated in the First Pillar of supranational policy-making in the Treaty of Amsterdam. Bendel argues how with the Treaty of Amsterdam, the European Community Treaty has increased its influence in areas such as asylum policy to

---

[115] Kostakopoulou D. 'European Union Citizenship: Writing the Future' *European Law Journal* Vo 13 No 5 September 2007 p 3
[116] Ibid
[117] Green S. 2007 p 102

such an extent that European law in this area is 'superior to national legislation.'[118] Moreover, 'national veto power on asylum policies within the European institutions was gradually reduced and the European Parliament's competences were extended.'[119] With regards to policies encouraging the integration of migrants, Article 13 of the Treaty of Amsterdam conferred the Council the power to take the appropriate action to prevent discrimination based on racial or ethnic origin.[120] As a result, the Council adopted the Directive on racial discrimination. The integration of immigrants was seen as essential by the Commission, which has the role to initiate policies. Antonio Vitorino, the EU's Justice and Home Affairs Commissioner stated that "it is essential to create a welcoming society and to recognise that integration is a two-way process involving adaptation on the part of both the immigrant and of the host society. The EU is by its very nature a pluralist society enriched by a variety of cultural and societal traditions...there must, therefore, be respect for cultural and social differences."[121]

The influence of the progressive-minded Commission and the Parliament has for now remained somewhat cut off from issues lined to immigration. It is true to say that the most important comprehensive integration policies such as integration into the labour market, education and nationality/citizenship are still controlled by national legislation. Progress in this respect has notoriously been very slow. For this reason the Hague Programme exhorted EU member states and institutions to build on common basic principles providing a coherent European framework on integration. Communitarisation is still partial and far from complete since the member states continue to insist on keeping their domestic competencies in these areas. As Geddes explains, "immigration and asylum were 'communitarised' in the sense that they moved to the Community pillar, but were not 'supranationalised' in the sense of being made subject to day-to-day process of integration."[122] Thus, the supranational level still plays a relatively narrow role and the European dimension has relatively limited effect on the domestic policy frameworks. The impact has been subtle, even though many EU member states face the same pressures and

---

[118] Bendel P. 2005 p 22
[119] Ibid
[120] Ibid
[121] Cited in Herz D. 'European Immigration and Asylum Policy-Scope and Limits of Intergovernmental Europeanization' *EUSA Conference* March 29 2003 p 10
[122] Geddes A. 2003 p 137

share some of the policy goals. Just recently, the current foreign minister of Italy and former vice-president of the European Commission, Franco Frattini, urged the European Union institutions to take stronger actions and to issue a new immigration policy as soon as possible since immigration is a 'European problem' and 'all 27 countries must bear responsibility.'[123] As Adrian Flavell points out, "the crystallisation of a truly European 'immigration regime' is on hold."[124] Yet, in spite of the inconsistencies in some areas, there have been fundamental developments since the pre-Maastricht era, which in time could lead to a European migration 'regime' or 'policy framework' that could allow the harmonisation of issues related to immigration such as citizenship laws and dual nationality. In the post-war era policies on immigration and issues such as the integration of ethnic minorities have always been considered as the exclusive responsibility of their European host nation. The successful process of European integration in the 1980s and 1990s have created new opportunities through an increased economic interdependence and open borders allowing the free movement of labour and people, and have encouraged EU member states to move towards a "more Europeanised common culture, founded on a political unity of multinational and multicultural citizenship rights."[125]

---

[123] Biondi P. 'EU to draft new immigration policy by October' *Reuters* August 23 2009
[124] Flavian A. 'The Europeanisation of immigration polictics' *European Integration online Papers* (EioP) Vol 2 N 10 1998 p 4
[125] Ibid p 2

Conclusion

Schroder's team has made some important steps toward the integration of immigrants such as introducing the principle of ius soli and facilitating the process of naturalisation. Together with the United Kingdom, Germany has granted more than sixty per cent of the total number of citizenships conferred by the twenty seven EU member states from 2002 to 2007.[126] The 'not a country of immigration' formula has receded from public discourse and the concept of citizenship has become more inclusive over the last few years. If the *Kein Einwanderungs Land* slogan has been gradually replaced by debates on whether to integrate or assimilate immigrants, yet the extent of the changes brought by the new legislations remains questionable for the ethnographic notion of citizenship still appears to be strongly embedded in German society. In the light of the Leitkultur debate and the rise of far right parties in the Eastern part of Germany, it might be too early to talk about a multicultural Germany. The *Ostdeutschen* are still in the process of adapting to a postmodern, capitalist and globalised world characterised by the increased interaction of people from all over the world. Moreover, in times of recession and economic crisis like the current one, high levels of unemployment ignite anti-immigrant sentiments. Thus, it is not surprising that a recent Allesbacher Berichte found out that only twenty three percent of Germans see multiculturalism in positive terms, arguing that foreigners constitute a threat to German identity and way of life.[127] The belief that immigrants should take on a German life style was support by 72 per cent of respondents in 2004 compared to 50 per cent in 1996.[128] Assimilation is still viewed as necessary to avoid the creation of parallel societies, which augment segregation. Cultural belonging and the adoption of German customs are still viewed as an essential prerequisite for a more extensive social and political participation. The view that 'immigrants with a diverse cultural background should not expect to be treated as Germans for they still have to become German' is still widespread. Studies have shown that the media sustains the negative discourse and reinforces the negative attitude of the population towards immigration: "Afternoon television talk shows, popular among the less educated youth and young adults, transmit as an outspoken message the concept of

---

[126] Vasileva K. & Sartori F. ,'Population and social conditions' *Eurostat Statistics in focus* 108 *2008* p 1
[127] Allensbacher Berichte, 'Multikulturelle Geselschaft' No. 9 http://www.ifd-allensbach.de/Seiten/Abericht.html Accessed on 5/11/08
[128] Ibid

distinct cultures and national traits. The media portrays immigrants rather as objects that cause problems for the receiving country."[129] Immigration is in fact still viewed by a large section of society as a source of social and cultural problems. It is hard to say how much integration the country is willing to have in the future since there is still no consensus on what the benefits and the costs of immigration are. It will always be different from the classic countries of multiculturalism such as the US due to its diverse historical tradition and path dependency. For many multicultural Germany will always sound like an oxymoron. The new citizenship reforms do not promote multiculturalism for they continue to focus on commonality rather than difference. There hasn't been a shift from a homogeneous form of thinking to a heterogeneous one. The German national model is still appears to be ethno-assimilationalist.

At the same time, the number of foreign residents in Germany is growing on a daily basis, particularly in the urban areas. Frankfurt, known as the economic capital and as well as a multicultural metropolis, reaches an average of over thirty per cent. In other cities including Stuttgart, Munich, Hamburg, Dusseldorf, and Cologne the proportion ranges from fifteen to over twenty-five per cent.[130] Germany will need to acknowledge the inevitable transformation in the long run of classical unitary and ethnically homogeneous societies into socio-cultural realities permanently characterised by an ethnically heterogeneous population. The transition will be gradual but essential for the well functioning and the unity of a modern liberal democratic civil society. The ethnocultural model defining citizenship as a concept rooted in the understanding of nationhood will most likely not endure in Europe. The SPD-Green government acknowledged the inevitable need to change this traditional model in a globalising society and introduced important innovations via the 2000 Nationality Act. However, granting dual citizenship is an essential prerequisite for a society with a well integrated immigrant population. The importance of lifting the restriction on dual citizenship was recently emphasized by the interior minister of Schleswig-Holstein, Ralf Stegner, who has recently urged the Merkel administration to review their position on the matter: "Those foreigners who are well-integrated, speak the German language and have an

---

[129] Cyrus N. & Vogel D. 'Germany' in Triandeafyllidou A. & Gropas R. 'European Immigration' (Ashgate 2007) p 137
[130] Kasper B., Reutter U. & Schubert S. 'Transport Behaviour among Immigrants- an Equation with many unknowns' *DFK* (Deutsche Zeitschrift fur Kommunalwissenschaften) Vo. 46 No. 2 2007 p 2

income of their own should be offered German citizenship....without the precondition of having to relinquish their original nationality first."[131] Of course the position of the CDU-CSU remains unaltered. Conservative leader Koch responded that "the majority population must be sure that applicants assimilate and accept German life as it is. Citizenship is a manifestation that should not be made easy and dual citizenship must remain an exception rather than the rule."[132] In spite of the unaltered position of the conservatives, important endogenous factors, especially demographic and skill shortages, may force the CDU/CSU to reconsider its stance on the integration of immigrants. The Europeanization of domestic politics and of national identity is also likely to have a structural impact. Risse points out how "there is no contractual obligation to develop a common European identity" and there are no "formal norms requiring EU citizens to transfer their loyalties to the EU instead of the nation-state."[133] However, if an increasing number of competences move to the EU level with a common decision-making via supranational institutions, the Europeanization of domestic policies on immigration would erode national sovereignty and challenge nation-state identities. The shifting of sovereignty to the transnational European level would have important consequences for the perception and understanding of national identity, which is the basis for the concept of citizenship and, most importantly, is not a static concept because it changes and develops historically. Thus, cultural assimilation could be brushed away and Germany could recast itself as a civic nation.

---

[131] Deutsche Welle 'German Minister Urges Reversal of Dual Citizenship Policy' 24.04.2007
[132] Ibid
[133] Risse T. 2001 p 200

Bibliography

- Allensbacher Berichte, 'Multikulturelle Geselschaft' No. 9
  http://www.ifd-allensbach.de/Seiten/Abericht.html Accessed on 5/7/09

- Anil M 'No More Foreigners? The remaking of German Naturalization and Citizenship Law, 1990-200' *Dialectical Anthropology* 29/ 3-4 2005

- Baubock R. Groenendijk K. Waldrauch H. 'Acquisition and Loss of Nationality' (2006 Amsterdam: Amsterdam University Press)

- BBC News 'Dwindling Germans review policies'March 2006
  http://news.bbc.co.uk/1/hi/world/europe/4852040.stm

- Bendel P. 'Immigration Policy in the European Union: Still bringing up the walls for fortress Europe?' Migration Letters Vo 2 N.1 April 2005

- Biondi P. 'EU to draft new immigration policy by October' *Reuters* August 23 2009

- Birnbaum R. 'Schauble : Doppelte Staatsburgerschaft ist Gift fur Die Integration' *Der Tagespiel* 4 January 1999

- Bommes M. & Geddes A. 'Immigration and Welfare: Challenging the Borders of the Welfare State (London: Routledge, 2000)

- Brubaker W.R. 'Citizenship and Nationhood in France and Germany' (1992, Cambridge, Mass: Harvard University Press)

- Brubaker R. ;The return to assimilation? Changing perspectives on immigration and its sequels in France, Germany, and the United States' *Ethnic and Racial Studies* Vo. 24 N. 4 July 2001

- Bulmer S.J. & Radaelli C.M. 'The Europeanisation of National Policy?' *Queen's Papers on Europeanisation* Vo. 1 2004

- Chapin D. W. 'Germany for the Germans? The Political Effects of International Migration' (1997, Greenwood Press: Westport)

- Carle R. 'Citizenship Debates in the New Germany' *Springer Scien*ce Vo. 44 August 2007

- Checkel T.J '(Regional) Norms and (Domestic) Social Mobilization: Citizenship Politics in Post-Maastricht, Post-Cold War Germany' *Arena Working* Papers 99/3 February 1999

- CSU 'Zehn Leitlinien fur eine gesetzliche Regelung zur Zuwanderung' (2000) http://www.csu.de

- Cyrus N. & Vogel D. 'Germany' in Triandeafyllidou A. & Gropas R. 'European Immigration' (Ashgate 2007)

- Day S. 'Dealing with Alien Suffrage: Ecamples from the EU and Germany' *Centre for the Study of Law in Europe* 22 May 2000

- Deutsche Welle 'Germany's Long Road to Multiculturalism' 21.07.2005

- Deutsche Welle 'German Minister Urges Reversal of Dual Citizenship Policy' 24.04.2007

- 'Deutschland: 15 Mio. Einwohner mit 'Migrationshintergrund' Migration und Bevolkerung 5 2006 http://www.migration-info.de/migration_und_bevoelkerung/artikel/060502.htm

- Doerschler P. 'Push-Pull Factors and Immigrant Political Integration in Germany' *Social Science Quarterly* Vo. 87 No. 5 December 2006

- Drieschner F. 'Ist Multikulti schuld?' Die Zeit nr 16 , 12/04/2006 http://www.zeit.de/2006/16/contra

- Eckardt F. 'Multiculturalsim in Germany: From Ideology to Pragmatism- and Back?' *National Identities* Vol. 9 No. 3 September 2007

- Eurostat '379.4 million inhabitants in the EU and 305.1 million in the euro zone on 1 January 2002' http://epp.eurostat.ec.europa.eu/cache/ITY_PUBLIC/3-11012002-AP/EN/3-11012002-AP-EN.HTML

- Faist T. & Ette A. 'The Europeanization of National Policies and Politics of Immigration' (New York, Palgrave Macmillan 2007)

- Flavian A. 'The Europeanisation of immigration polictics' *European Integration online Papers* (EioP) Vol 2 N 10 1998

- Geddes A. 'The Politics of Migration and Immigration in Europe' (London,Sage Publications: 2003)

- Gerhard Schroder speech 10 November 1998 , *German Information Center* http://www.germany.info/relaunch/politics/speeches/111098.html

- Green S. 'Beyond ethnoculturalsim? German citizenship in the new millenium' *German Politics* 9:3 2000

- Green S, 'Immigration, asylum and citizenship in Germany: The impact of unification and the Berlin republic,' *West European Politics*, Vo. 29 No. 1, 1 October 2001

- Green S. Cited in Padgett S.; Paterson W.E.; Smith G. 'Developments in German politics'(London: Palgrave Macmillan 2003)

- Green S. 'The politics of exclusion: Institutions and immigration policy in contemporary Germany' (2004, Manchester University Press)

- Green S. 'Divergent Traditions, Converging Responses: Immigration and Integration Policy in the UK and Germany', *German Politics* 16/1 2007

- Hammar T. 'Comparing European and North American International Migration', *International Migration View*, Vo. 23 No. 3 (1989)

- Hansen-Thomas H. 'Language ideology, citizenship, and identity: The case of modern Germany' *Journal of Language and Politics* 6:2 (2007)

- Hansen R. & Koehler J. 'Issue Definition, Political Discourse and the Politics of Nationality Reform in France and Germany' European Journal of Political Research 44/5 (2005)

- Heckmann Friedrich 'From Ethnic Nation to Universalistic Immigrant Integration: Germany' edited by Heckman F. & Schnapper D. 'The integration of immigrants in European societies' EFMS (2003, Lucius: Stuttgart)

- Herz D. 'European Immigration and Asylum Policy-Scope and Limits of Intergovernmental Europeanization' *EUSA Conference* March 29 2003

- Heywood. P. Et al, 'Developments in European Politics,' (London,2006: Palgrave Macmillan)

- Howard M.M. 'The Causes and Consequences of Germany's New Citizenship Law' *German Politics* Vo. 17 No. 1 March 2008

- Huntington S. 'The Clash of Civilizations?' *Foreign Affairs*, Vo. 72, No. 3 (Summer 1993)

- Joppke C. 'Multiculturalism and Immigration' *Theory and Society* 25, 1996

- Joppke C. 'Why Liberal States Accept Unwanted Immigration' *World Politics* 50.2 1998

- Joppke C. 'Immigration and the Nation-State' (Oxford: Oxford University Press,1999)

- Joppke C. 'Selecting By Origin' (Cambridge: Harvard University Press, 2005)

- Kahanec M. & Tosun M.S. 'Political Economy of Immigration in Germany: Attitudes and Citizenship Aspirations' *Institute for the Study of Labour (IZA)* No 3140 November 2007

- Kasper B., Reutter U. & Schubert S. 'Transport Behaviour among Immigrants– an Equation with many unkowns' *DFK* (Deutsche Zeitschrift fur Kommunalwissenschaften) Vo. 46 No. 2 2007

- Klopp B.'German Multiculturalism: Immigrant Integration and the Transformation of Citizenship' (Westport: Praeger Publishers, 2002)

- Koopmans R. & Statham P. 'Migration and ethnic relations as a field of political contention: An opportunity structure approach' in Koopman R. & Statham P. 'Challenging Immigration and Ethnic Relations Politics: Comparative European Perspective' (2000,Oxford: Oxford University Press)

- Kostakopoulou D. 'European Union Citizenship: Writing the Future' *European Law Journal* Vo 13 No 5 September 2007

- Kruse I; Orren E.H. ;Angenendt S. 'The failure of immigration reform in Germany' *German Politics* 1 December 2003

- Layton-Henry Z. 'Citizenship and Migrant Workers in Western Europe' in Vogel U. & Moran M. 'The Frontiers of Citizenship' (Houndmills: Macmillan, 1991)

- Madel R. ' Fortress Europe and the Foreigners Within: Germany's Turks' in Goddard V.A. & Llobera J.R. and Shore C. The Anthropology of Europe (Oxford: Berg, 1994)

- Neuman G. 'Nationality Law in the United States and Germany' in Schuck P. & Munz R. 'In paths to Inclusion: The integration of Migrants in the United States and Germany' (1998, Providence: Berghan Books)

- Neuman G.L. 'National Law as a Method of Integration – A Comparison Between the USA and Germany' draft chapter

- Pautz H. 'The politics of identity in Germany : the *Leitkultur* debate' *Race and Class* Vo. 46 N. 4, 2005

- Parekh B. 'Rethinking Multiculturalism' (New York: Palgrave Macmillan 2006)

- Peters G. 'Institutional Theory in Political Science: The New Institutionalism' (London, 1999: Pinter)

- Prumm K. & Alscher S. 'The Europeanization of National Policies and Politics of Immigration' in Faist T. and Ette A. 'The Europeanization of National Policies and Politics of Immigration' (New York: Palgrave Macmillan 2007)

- Risse 'A European Identity' in Cowles G.M.; Caporaso J.; Risse T.' Transforming Europe' (Cornell: Cornell University Press, 2001)

- Savage M. 'Baby boom drives British population to record high' *The Independent* 28 August 2009

- Scholte J.A. 'Globalisation: a critical introduction' (2005, London: Palgrave Macmillan)

- Schonbohm J. *Junge Freiheit* (19 March 1997)

- Schonbohm J. *Berliner Morgenpost* (24 April 1997)

- Statistiches Bundesamt Deutschland 'Foreign population' 2009

- The Economist 'Two unamalgamated worlds', April 5th 2008

- Thielemann E. 'The Soft Europeanisation of Migration Policy European Integration and Domestic Policy Challenge' ECSA Seventh Biennial International Conference, May 31– June 2, 2001

- Thranhardt D. 'Germany's Immigration Policies and Politics' in Brochman G. And Hammar t. 'Mechanisms of Immigration control: A Comparative Analysis of European Regulation Policies' (Oxford:1999)

- Vasileva K. & Sartori F. ,'Population and social conditions' *Eurostat Statistics in focus* 108 *2008*

- Vink M. 'Negative and Positive Integration in European Immigration Policies'European Integration online Papers (EIoP) Vo. 6 N. 13 August 2002

- Von Stritzky J. 'Germany's Immigration Policy: From Refusal to Reluctance' *ARI* 93 3/6/2009

- Vogel, Dita:, 'Migration control in Germany and the United States' *International Migration Review* Vo. 34, No. 2 2000

- Woods R. 'Germany's New Right as culture and politics'(London: Palgrave Macmillan, 2007)